THE CURVY GIRLS STYLE HANDBOOK

SUZE SOLARI

Claymore Ulfberht & Xiphos LLC

To my husband Joe and sons, Rowan and Vincent, who with their love and encouragement, made this project a reality.

To the readers of my first two books, who asked for my help in representing them and for the resources to feel amazing in their clothes.

FOREWORD

Clothes are the deepest expression of our individuality, they should give us the bold confidence to express exactly who we are and what we stand for.

When it comes to feeling comfortable in our own skin and being stylish at the same time, I know it can sometimes be... well, a challenge! Between finding the right clothes to fit our bodies and discovering our own personal style, getting dressed can often feel like more of a chore than fun.

Let's change that.

INTRODUCTION

This handbook is not your typical fashion style guide, where you struggle to relate as I speak about the latest fashion trends of Paris, London, or L.A., leaving you trying to figure out how to incorporate these into your wardrobe. There will be no lithe, fresh-skinned models smiling on the streets of Milan, in garments that haven't even hit the stores yet.

I am so passionate about this project; it is a love letter to every woman who has ever felt bad about her body and her style. It's all about celebrating and relating to the everyday woman, with an understanding that the looks featured here are attainable by using clothes bought from regular stores, and not necessarily the latest season fashions.

How this book can help you, is by demonstrating ways to upgrade what you already have, to fully express your personal style. By evaluating the structure of your clothes and using my two key styling principles, I call the 'V for Victory', and the 'B for put a belt on it' and other strategies, you will learn how to create shapes that flatter and celebrate your curves, as opposed to concealing them.

If you are not sure what your style is, or you feel like you lost your style underneath a child's car seat years ago, I can show you how to regain it. Not by spending thousands of dollars on new clothes, or forcing you through some Zen closet cleanse, but through utilizing what is in your closet right now.

Don't get me wrong, I hope that along the way we clean up some unhelpful clutter. Let's begin by smashing one widely held misconception. One that if you don't overtly believe, it dwells in your subconscious.

In researching this book, I asked my newsletter list to take a short survey. One question was "What is your perception of your size?" Sixty-eight percent of the respondents answered bigger than average. Later, I asked for the person's actual size, so I could discern the difference between the perception and reality. Only five percent of the respondents were bigger than the average size 16. In fact, the results showed that thirty-one percent of those who completed the survey were a size 16 and sixty nine percent fell between 12- 16.

The reality is that eighty percent of the respondents are average size or smaller, but the voice in their head is messaging that they are big.

You are not the problem; the fashion industry is. Think about how broken a business is, to tell the majority of its customers that they are wrong and need to change.

Here is an example of how that frustration has been expressed to me. I was sent this email from a reader of my first two books.

Subject: Help, I am tired of frumpy, ill-fitting, and uncomfortable options

On Jul 10, 2017, at 6:50 P.M, MM wrote:

I love your books, I hate your books. While I have learned a lot, I feel that most of the information does not address everyone. For instance, I am a plus size, 5 ft 4.5 inches, look like an apple, and have a very hard time buying every piece of clothing, from bras to shoes.

Pants are always mis-proportioned, if they fit at the waist then there is room for another person in the rear and hips, there is only so much a tailor can do.

Your first book did not address what an apple should look for in jeans. Forget shoes. I tried on every sandal in the department store, and all were too narrow.

And bras, ugh, the straps always fall down, the sides just give me a muffin top under my arms and back, and the back rides up. While I like the visuals and the information on what makes a good outfit, I am discouraged about my prospects for finding a simple white T-shirt that looks good.

Could I lose weight? Ideally yes, but you know what, I am 62 years old, have dieted all my life and I am tired of that struggle. Could I pay someone like yourself to help? Not on a teacher's salary. I figure (pun intended) at least I could learn how to dress well.

I am hoping that sometime in the future you write a book for all of us forgotten women, I like your practical approach. Thanks for letting me vent, there are a lot of us out there......

Respectfully,

MM

So, with this inspiration in mind, I set out to give you a different experience.

The models are real women:

If you don't see yourself in these women, then they likely will remind you of one of your friends. There is a cross-section of ages, ethnicities, and body shapes. All the models are women I have come across who have voiced similar issues with clothing options, needed to regain their style, or faced wardrobe issues because of the careers they have.

These amazing women have also shared their stories here and I bet you will see similarities in the challenges you face and some misconceptions you labor under.

The clothes are real:

Rather than the typical look-book where clothing brands supply clothes in an effort to influence you to buy them, I started with each model's own closet. I put together outfits from their clothes and one or two borrowed items from some friends of mine, to create our inspiring Looks section. Think about that what I said. You can do something similar without buying a thing, just by going into your own closet and perhaps swapping some things with friends.

Anyone can look amazing if a Lucky Brand representative, for example, spent two hours preparing and styling them for a photo shoot. At a typical magazine fashion shoot, the clothing company selects people (models) who are best suited for the clothes; the exact opposite of what we do when buying new clothes. They have hand selected an outfit directly from the factory, then custom fitted it for that professional model. Hairstyling and make-up is applied (usually two different artists) before a professional photo shoot; afterward, photoshop and airbrush touch-ups are applied. This is how the photos are produced for magazine layouts, catalogs, and online shopping websites. They are highly produced, unrealistic and in complete opposition to what we wanted to achieve for this book.

We hired an amazing, creative to photograph our models. She and I spent 90 minutes on each model, who did their own hair & makeup. Like I said, the looks you see here came from the models' own closet and include pieces that they either only ever wore one way, or never wore because they struggled with how to wear it. Each model has at least four looks to address the four seasons.

About my why: what a wonderful world it will be when we all decide to love and accept ourselves just the way we are. This is absolutely possible, and I want to be a part of it, so this book is my love letter to all the amazing women who feel invisible, or forgotten by our culture, by the apparel and fashion industry or by themselves. We are not going to take it anymore.

I know my purpose on the planet, my epic mission if you will, and it is to help people heal, dang it! I want women to feel confident in their physical, mental, emotional and environmental bodies every day… and the conduit I use to make this happen is the wardrobe.

My inspiration is YOU. The goal is to provide a useful guide for all of you badass, hard-working women out there, to create an environment where we all feel empowered, loved and fabulous in our clothes. I hope that this resource will give you the tools to get dressed every day in comfort, style, and confidence.

CHAPTER 1: MY STORY

Growing up in Portland Oregon, the grunge capital of the world in the 1990's, and pretty much still is, with a good dose of DIY thrown in; I was not exposed to high fashion of any kind, but I did cultivate my love of vintage at an early age.

My body type is petite curvy, with an emphasis on petite, meaning: short. I am usually one of the shortest people in any room, and have to admit it has not always been easy dealing with the comments: 'wow, you really are short', etc., 'are you old enough to be in here?', etc. I definitely had to constantly prove my age, (which is working pretty good for me now) but more importantly, I felt I had to constantly prove my value.

After graduation from design school, I worked for a west coast department store in the interior construction division. My colleagues were professionals of all ages, on average over 15 years older than me; male and female. During my college years I gained an extra 15 pounds, and in this working environment, I found it difficult to disguise the weight. I could no longer hide behind baggy sweat-shirts and leggings (this was 1989, how fashion history does repeat). I needed to upgrade my style quickly to fit in, and command respect as a project manager; running site meetings and working in an office with a large department of Engineers, Construction Managers, and other Interior Designers.

I worked alongside two very slim and stylish female colleagues, my professional mentors. I recall looking at them longingly every day.

"If only I could have a flat stomach", I lamented.

And so, I began my years of dieting and over-exercising. I got a membership to the YMCA and became a slave to step aerobics. I wore one those stupid leotards with the thong and hated that step class. I limited my food intake, and started drinking weak, tasteless coffee, this was just before Starbucks expanded to Portland and then took over the world. At least after that, I had yummy coffee to drink.

There was another junior member of our team who was thin and beautiful. She had the most enviable body shape, and received head-turning looks at every moment, it seemed. I wondered how she could eat a whole plate of eggs, bagels, hash-browns, and wear a size 2, while I chewed on half a piece of dry wheat toast?

So, I dieted more and joined another, more trendy gym and continued to struggle to lose weight and look a certain way. Being 5' – 1" and high waisted, I believed even a small amount of excess weight was horrifying and could not get the thought out of my head that I was fat. I weighed 125, the most I had ever weighed, and wore a size 6/8. I had success with expensive prepared food programs, like Nutra-Systems, but the pounds kept coming back, even while I paid a lot of money for their 'maintenance programs'.

It was not until I lived in Hong Kong and Singapore that things changed. The lifestyle in these two Asian cities is almost exclusively pedestrian based. Most people do not own cars; not only are they very expensive to buy and taxed to put on the road, they are quite unnecessary. Mass transit systems including underground rail, buses, and cable cars that made it convenient to access all parts of the city and territories by public transportation and walking. I worked for several international interior design and build companies, designing and fitting out commercial office and retail spaces. So, I walked everywhere for 5 years, took the MTR (public transportation), from my office, to and from clients and site visits.

I have no scientific basis to back this up, but I believe I changed my metabolic set point, and shed those pounds I had always had trouble with. More importantly, I have found a balance with my body, including a pregnancy with twins, that is comfortable and long-lasting.

However, I still struggle to find harmony with the right cut and proportions with the clothes I buy and wear. Even though I have an instinct for style and love of fashion, I have to scrutinize garments and accessories closely, evaluating if the fit is right for my short torso, long arms and fussy feet.

Can the straps be taken up, and still leave me a comfortable armhole? Will the instep accommodate my orthotics? Dresses are nearly impossible for me to fit comfortably, especially those with a built-in waistband. So, I create my own waistbands, by removing those little loops and utilze my own belts to create definition at my waist. **By using my 'B' strategy, I manipulate the structure of the dress, to highlight my natural waistline.**

The challenges I face being so short, have affected not only my self - confidence but my budget. Alteration on pants is nearly always a given. My feet arches are extremely high and have caused back and foot pain since I can remember, when my first job as a waitress required me to be on my feet for hours.

In my effort to appear taller, I look for shoes with a platform to add height; however, I can not wear a shoe with an incline of over 2 inches. Additionally, I look for block heels and molded footbeds; I use orthotics to put into my boots, and purchase arch inserts to go into mules and sandals that don't accommodate the orthotics. This routine can be expensive and time-consuming. I almost always bring two pairs of shoes wear ever I go, affording me the mobility of a supportive flat for commuting, and a quick change in the elevator for my preferred shoe!

When my kids were two years old and I could finally get myself out of the house regularly, I began making jewelry again and selling them at art fairs. Also, in my desire to get the creative juices flowing again, I started an interior design business, helping people reconfigure their bedrooms, basements and playrooms, etc.

Spending time in their boudoirs, and observing the state of their belongings gave me a serious pause. I could not leave their houses until I understood why they stored Halloween candy, Christmas presents, and all sorts of clutter amongst their clothing. They could not find mates to shoes, clothes were on the floor, jewelry and other accessories, scattered. I wanted to help, and I found doing so to be fun and rewarding; hence, the birth of my personal style consultancy.

Along the way, I wrote some books on the subject of style, for women, with a focus on the basic pieces that most of us are comfortable wearing. This resulted in two books on how to upgrade your personal style, called: The T-Shirt & Jeans Handbook and The Blouse & Skirt Handbook.

Both books are for women who are busy juggling family and work and want to feel feminine and be more creative with their wardrobe. The handbooks cover everything from which T-shirts and jeans, blouses and skirts look good on what body shapes, where to find them, and how to create chic outfits with fun and ease.

It is my intention with this new book, that you gain an understanding of how to have the optimal components in your closet; the right silhouettes, fit and proportion for your body shape, making getting dressed every day joyful, timely and productive, in addition to tapping into that most authentic and amazing expression of yourself.

CHAPTER 2: BODY SHAPE BREAKDOWN

And why it's important to know for getting dressed

T hree hundred years ago when kings and rich guys went to the best artists to commission paintings for the trendiest decorations for their latest castle, they expected to see something like the image below. They did not call these women pears or apples; the term coined was Rubenesque, and it was synonymous with hot! Sure, these paintings were allegorical and intellectual, but they were also erotic. Famous Flemish painter, Peter Paul Rubens painted similar compositions, all showing the front, side and back of a woman, so you could see all of her curves.

The Three Graces 1630-35 Peter Paul Rubens

So, if you are prepared to give up electricity and modern medicine, you could live in a time where your body shape was idealized. Now, we have added one more thing about your body image that is also out of your control, the century you were born into.

If you are one of those people beating yourself up about your inability to alter your Rubenesque shape, let's look at those who have worked themselves into top levels of athletic achievement.

There are women who, through functional fitness, have achieved the peak of human performance. Each year Crossfit crowns the fittest woman on the planet. What these contestants are capable of is quite amazing and inspiring.

Along with this fitness movement comes another opportunity to redefine body image. While these women may be very proud of their abilities and their bodies, they still do not fit into fashion's current archetype and struggle with the cut and silhouette of their garments. They too are not well served by the fashion and apparel industry.

The conclusion goes back to what we learned from my survey. Society has such a pervasive impact on our psyche, that which we perceive and that which is true. An average woman feels that she is not normal because of the images projected on her. Now, as new body archetypes develop, such as the Crossfitter body, don't expect the fashion industry to respond or respect those needs either.

Many people think that "body type" just describes the way someone looks. In fact, your body type can also provide information about how you respond to food intake and about your hormonal and sympathetic nervous system characteristics.

Physique characteristics can thus be linked to metabolic differences between individuals. Once someone establishes their body type, they can then adjust nutrient intake to maximize body composition and health-related goals.

There are three general categories of body types (somatotypes): ectomorph, mesomorph, and endomorph.

Very few people fall perfectly into one of the three categories. People are often a mix of characteristics. Additionally, years of training and good nutrition can change the outward appearance of one's body.

For instance, a bodybuilder might be mistaken for a "natural" mesomorph when in fact, she is really an endomorph who has trained and dieted hard; or an ectomorph who has spent years guzzling protein shakes and performing power lifts.

An ectomorph who has gained a little weight around the middle from a sedentary lifestyle and poor nutrition might assume they're more endomorphic.

However, most folks can find their general tendencies in one of the three groups.

Ectomorphs are thin individuals, characterized by smaller bone structures and thinner limbs. Think of a typical endurance athlete. These folks are linked to a fast metabolic rate and a high carbohydrate tolerance.

Mesomorphs have a medium sized bone structure and athletic body, and if they're active, they usually have a considerable amount of lean mass. Many explosive athletes like wrestlers and gymnasts fit these criteria. This profile leads to a predisposition for muscle gain and the maintenance of a lower body fat.

Endomorphs, AKA Curvy Girls!

Endomorphs have a larger bone structure with higher amounts of total body mass and fat mass. They tend to have a naturally lower metabolism. Where the ectomorphs tend to burn off excess calories even without movement, excess calories in an endomorph seem to stick around.

This means that excess calories are more likely to be stored as fat. This profile leads to a greater propensity for energy storage, including both lean mass and fat mass. This can also mean a lower carbohydrate tolerance.

Most of us can slot our overall body shape into one of these categories, recognizing that there are wide varieties of builds and sizes within each group.

Knowing your body composition can be quite liberating because it gives you something to focus on in a good way; that no matter what the scale says, if you are in a healthy body composition range, you're all good! Now, let's have some fun and get right into the looks.

CHAPTER 3: THE LOOKS

C urves are real — and they're spectacular! You can achieve success by knowing your own personal style and applying it to getting dressed every day, no matter where you go or what you do. If clothing can help us see ourselves at our very best, why shouldn't every day be that day?

This section is intended to guide you visually through photos of my curvy models, real women who love to dress up, and dress down; to look and most importantly, feel amazing in their outfits every day.

Every body shape is different, if you're not one of these shapes— that's ok. These dressing guidelines are best utilized as a starting point to understanding the basics. And, let's be honest, most women are a combination of several. It's all about mixing and matching until you find what works best for you and helps you to get excited about dressed and feeling fabulous.

In the introduction, I suggested that we can use the structure of our clothes and utilize my two key styling principles, I call the **'V for victory'**, and the **'B, for put a belt on it'**, to create a feminine shape that follows our celebrated curves. When we hide it, we have no shape, feel boxy, heavier energetically, and this is not flattering. I quite often hear from clients who tell me, 'I have no waist'. Well, everyone does, but if yours does not have as much definition as you would like it to, you can create the shape for yourself using these principals.

The 'V for victory' neckline emphasizes the hourglass shape, by reducing the volume of a large bust line, making your shoulders look wider, and waist narrower. A button down top, or a blazer, for example, naturally create a V – shape, you can also suggest it with accessories like a long necklace or a scarf.

Go -To Items for creating this shape:

• Scarf

• Long necklace(s) yes, more than one at a time

• Fitted blazer

• Long draped cardigan

• Wrap dress

The 'B, for put a belt on it' styling strategy is another visual aid for creating more definition at the waistline. This is why all women look good in a classic 'fit and flare' dress, because it reinforces the hourglass form.

Go -To Items:

• Self - belted dress, or fit n' flare dress
• Belts : thin and medium in width, in leather – black, brown, tan and metallic; woven and link chains; gold and silver
• Peplum tops: a top that has a fitted waist and flared hem

By adopting these visual concepts, in addition to my other styling strategies, you can start to shift the things in your closet and regain your power by incorporating all of your clothes into 'new and improved' outfits.

And, I believe the best place to really get the lowdown on how to dress for your body is from *real* women — just like you. Commonly, the women here have found their sizes to be a combination of several; to put this into context for you, their sizes run from a 6 to an 18, which makes up eighty percent of the average size of American women.

DENISE WALSH

My Story: As a Mexican woman, I'm naturally curvy. For much of my life, I have struggled with my weight, experiencing phases of being slim or heavy. This struggle can make it difficult to find the right clothes to wear. These body insecurities have impacted my social activities over the years, as it was easier to just hang out at home than to be seen.

Nearly 15 years ago, I stopped dieting and changed my lifestyle by choosing to eat healthier and start a regular exercise program. These new choices led to feeling better and having more energy. Although my weight can still fluctuate, I'm more accepting of my curves and make different choices to get back on track as needed.

Over the last year, I began a beauty business, selling long-lasting skincare and cosmetics that really work. Starting this business forced me to put myself out there and show the "real" me. I began going live on Facebook to demonstrate our products, so there were times when I didn't have any make-up on my face, not even lipstick. This exposure was scary at first, but the support of my friends and family has shown me others accept me as I am. Once I exposed my naked face, I decided I could expose my closet too, so Suze came over to help. In a short time, she created new ways for me to wear my clothes. Opening up my closet showed me that I'm not being judged but accepted by most people out there. It immediately changed my attitude and for the first time ever, I'm loving my curves. I want to wear what makes me feel comfortable and good about myself; these days I stand taller and smile brighter.

Denise Walsh **Look: Winter**

Outfit 1 Winter:

- Graphic floral skirt
- Grey knit top
- Taupe trench coat
- Brown tall boots
- Gold and tan layered necklaces

It was love at first sight for Denise when she bought this mid-length skirt, intending to add more pattern into her wardrobe. However, when she got home, she actually felt stumped by the print, and only wore it with a black blouse … kind of boring. In addition, she prefers not to tuck in tops; she is slightly short in the waist and does not want to call attention to her mid-section.

This happens all the time, and why many of my clients tell me they only wear about 20 percent of their wardrobe, or wear each garment only one way. I suggested we could pull inspiration from the brown and grey in the print, to liven up the outfit, from the things Denise had in her closet.

We paired her V neck, '2 – way top', which establishes the **'V for victory'** shape at the neckline. From local Chicago designer, ME Majamas, the knit top works perfectly; fitted at the bust and neckline, but falls slightly A-line at the hem. This way, Denise can leave the top untucked, and still achieve a polished look.

Denise had several black cardigans and blazers to layer on top, but we wanted to give the look a freshness, and avoid black. We found this CABI brand, taupe, trench coat from resale shop, Trends, in Oak Park, IL. There are few better options than a fitted trench to bring together a sophisticated and professional look. Because the jacket is unlined, she can wear it indoors, left unbelted as we show it – almost like a robe, and it provides a narrowing silhouette. Of course, she can button the jacket and **'B for belt it'**, to help define her waist and use it for outer wear too.

Layering two necklaces is one of my favorite styling strategies for creating 'new' looks with the things you own. Here, we matched the brown tones in Denise's skirt with a J.Crew, topaz, crystal necklace and a faux ivory, vintage beaded necklace from Peggy Goodman Collection. Lastly, our resourceful model unearthed this vintage pair of brown leather, tall boots, that she thought she had given away, thinking they were 'too old'. But in fact, the chunky heel and slightly patent finish to the boot are not only back on trend, they are so comfy, she can wear them all day. Tip: avoid a 'too square' toe box if possible, this style from the 90's is not flattering. A round or pointed (i.e.: cowboy boots) is timeless.

Denise Walsh   **Look: Spring**

Outfit 2 Spring:

- Straight Jeans
- Turquoise jersey knit, boat neck top
- Black open knit kimono
- Grey and black patent leather pump shoe
- Pearl, pyrite and aqua quartz, long strand necklace

Denise told me she most frequently wears dresses, but occasionally likes to wear jeans, especially if she is spending time with her little granddaughter. She had this pair of straight leg jeans, which is a good go – to for a classic look. She could also wear a flare hem, to give her a balanced silhouette for her body type. The turquoise scoop neck, jersey top is such a great choice for Denise's Latina skin; and in fact, one color that looks amazing on any skin tone. The **'V-shape'** is created by layering on a long, beaded necklace.

Most people who know me, can confirm that I am obsessed with kimonos! These fabulous, body skimming pieces can be worn casually with a T-shirt like our crochet version here from Calypso brand, or more dressed up, with the choice of fabrics like silk and yes, sequins too.

Denise Walsh   **Look: Summer**

Outfit 3 Summer:

- Red, cotton floral, maxi dress
- Denim jean jacket
- Gold & silver sandal
- Baroque pearl lariat

Ah, there is no end to the allure of a full - length dress. Not only is a maxi dress super comfortable, it's seriously sexy – not in an overt way of course, but with confidence. Add the bonus that we don't have to wear self -tanner or worry about shaving our legs, and I am so very much in!

This dress is fitted at the waist, creating our **'B, for put a belt on it'** style principal, and the slight A-line cut creates a super flattering line, making it easy for Denise to walk in. We chose a cream leather, block heel sandal she has had for years, that still look trés chic today. The **'Victory'** shape neckline is present here too.

Toss on a denim, jean jacket and the outfit instantly feels casual. We chose a baroque pearl lariat from Peggy Goodman Collections, to tie together the cream print in the dress and the shoes. Repeating a color or color tones, (meaning, it doesn't have to be an exact match) three times in the entire outfit is the trick to this layering technique.

Denise Walsh   **Look: Fall 1**

Outfit 4 Fall:

- Grey and blue floral dress
- Dark navy wide leg trouser
- Black knit vest
- Snake skin and patent leather shoes
- Silver fringe necklace

No matter how much effort you put into an outfit; and hopefully these images will inspire you to find it effortless; your love for every piece of clothing and accessory in your closet should be significant. Denise had an emotional good feeling when she bought this dress, and I was excited to help her wear it in a new way. Using the architecture of her clothing: the button down upper portion of the dress, Denise creatively implements the **'Victory'** neckline.

We shopped together for a wide leg trouser in a dark navy fluid fabric and paired it with the dress, using it as tunic. A vintage, medium size, bejeweled belt from Henri Bendel, adds panache and cinches in her waist, **'B for belt-line'.**

The patent leather and snake skin print are a forever, trend-less staple for her shoe choice, an adorable sling back style from Tahari and the necklace adds a little more texture to the ensemble. We gave Denise the option of wearing her black knit, swing vest for added warmth, but the soft draped quality establishes a narrowing silhouette by drawing the eye down the center of her body. Either way, Denise is truly feeling this outfit; how beautiful is she?

Denise Walsh   **Look: Fall 2**

STACEY SAUNDERS

My Story: I can't remember a time when I didn't have curves. I developed early and didn't really enjoy my body. My mom kept telling me my boobs were too big, and boys kept fidgeting with my bra during school. It was uncomfortable, and I didn't like it. Growing up, there a strong push to cover up and to find appropriate clothing. The message I got was to hide. Now, as a woman in her 40s, I feel the message is to show off my boobs and revel in their magnificence.

Three years ago, I decided to go out on my own after ten years in the corporate world. Starting my business, I could no longer hide behind a desk as I was now the face of my business, meeting and connecting with people. I wanted clothes that matched my personality. Suze helped me redefine what it meant to look professional upping my style game. I also learned that being professional can include color. Besides being a woman of color, I had none in my wardrobe. Lots of black and grey. Suze also opened my eyes to accessories. I now have an array of colors, not only in my clothes but my earrings, bracelets, and necklaces. She created outfits for me that can quickly go from day to night, to match my active lifestyle and highlight my best features. I'm definitely having more fun being flirty in my clothes.

Stacey Saunders　　　　**Look: Winter**

Outfit 1 Winter:

- White shift dress
- Cream and black cape, with faux fur collar
- Opaque patterned, dark brown tights
- Black riding boot

A cape is a truly useful article of clothing, helping to bridge from one season to the next. It also provides a layer of coverage over anything with extra fabric, which might feel binding under a winter coat. Sometimes, we just want to put winter off, as many of us who live in colder climates might agree.

If you want to try wearing a cape, keep the rest of the outfit simple in construction, and classic in aesthetic. Do make sure to coordinate the colors of the cape into your ensemble, like we did with Stacey's beautiful white shift dress, from Hugo Boss, at Nordstrom Rack. This stunning dress is very comfortable for Stacey to wear all day, and provides the perfect base for building our masterpiece. I often say that making outfits is like sculpture, applying a layered palette of texture, color, and pattern.

Stacey's cream, brown and black striped, wool cape trimmed in faux fur is super fun and chic. We kept the other elements subtle: textured tights and a black riding boot, great for all day; gold and tan jewelry to compliment her 'V for Victory' neckline.

Stacey Saunders   **Look: Winter**

Stacey Saunders   **Look: Spring 2**

Outfit 2 Spring:

- Coral wrap dress
- Camel draped, knit vest
- Tan and magenta, snakeskin, peep toe pumps
- Gold necklace and graphic cuff bracelet

When Stacey and I first started working together, she simply did not have enough clothes, and color barely existed in her closet outside of work-out wear. I am so excited to see her rocking this stunning jersey (a.k.a, comfort fiber) wrap dress in beautiful bright coral.

The wrap dress, made famous by Diane von Furstenberg in the 1970's, continues to be a prolific wardrobe workhorse today, and always looks good because of the **'Victory'** neckline and the automatic **'B'** waist-cinching wrap profile.

Pretty for the day, combined with a tan, knit swing vest, and light gold jewelry; also, elegant enough for a cocktail affair, paired with these stunning pink and tan peep-toe, Stuart Weitzman pumps, we found together at Nordstrom Rack.

Stacey Saunders   **Look: Summer**

Outfit 3 Summer:

- Floral, sheer top
- Cream camisole
- Teal cardigan
- Dark straight jeans
- Charcoal leather flats
- Bold silver earrings

Stacey's pretty smile is infectious, and her patterned top in blue tones bring added color to those pearly whites! We love that the blouse has a built-in **'Victory'** shaped neckline. It is further highlighted by an X in the tops' detail, and stunning turquoise crystal necklace, also following the **'V'** contour.

This sleeveless blouse is such a winner, as additionally, it has a built-in **'B for belt-line'** strategy, created by the folded hem, resembling a tucked in silhouette. Paired with a dark teal, draped cardigan, that … you guessed it, creates a narrowing image. A comfy silver metallic flat with a contoured sole will take Stacey from the wee hours of the morning, throughout the day and into the evening if need be, to accommodate her hectic work schedule.

Stacey Saunders   **Look: Fall**

Outfit 4 Fall:

- Grey silk top
- Dark rinse straight jeans
- Checked long jacket,
- Woolen faux fur duster – vest
- Black & floral stacked heal Maryjane shoes
- Silver jewelry

You had me at fur trimmed! It might be my second favorite garment type after a kimono, a duster vest (with pockets) this one is stunning, in an eye-catching maroon, woolen fabric. Stacey's ensemble actually began with the long, houndstooth jacket she loves from CABI; we like to belt it. A blazer is one garment that guarantees a pulled together, waist-defining look, with an automatic 'V' shape built in with a traditional lapel. Just pair it with anything, and you have an instant - cool professional look.

A simple dark, trouser jean, and neutral, white blouse comprise the base of this fabulous and fun outfit! We know Stacey is on her feet most days, so a block heel, Maryjane shoe in a cute black and floral fabric is a smart choice.

CONSTANCE CONTURSI BARKER

My story: Working in the fitness industry, people think I am natu-rally athletic and have never had to struggle with losing weight or keeping it off. I'm going to share with you one of the reasons I believe I have been so successful in my career… and that is because I am relatable.

First, as a kid, I failed gym class multiple times. How? Well, I hated it. It was boring, I was lazy, hated to sweat, always "forgot" my gym clothes and dodgeball was THE worst! Even my own friends wouldn't pick me to be on their teams in gym class. Like, I was THE last one picked…that's how un-athletic I was!

Second, I was 99 lbs. before I got pregnant with my first child and gained 80 lbs with her! When she was born I couldn't figure out how she was only 6 lbs. What about the other 74 lbs.? Well, my friends, this is where my weight loss journey began. This is where the blood, sweat and tears and dedication to working out came. I'll never forget thinking, "I can't wait 'till I'm back in shape, so that I can quit working out"… then I realized that I come from an Italian and Greek lineage whose bodies are made to be 300 pounds and that this HAS truly got to be a lifestyle change, otherwise I will end up like all of them- unhealthy, overweight and miserable about it.

If you stop, you go backward, you get comfortable and then the struggle gets real again. THIS is what led me to fitness and makes me understand the struggle all of my clients and members have and helps me to motivate them all appropriately and compassionately!

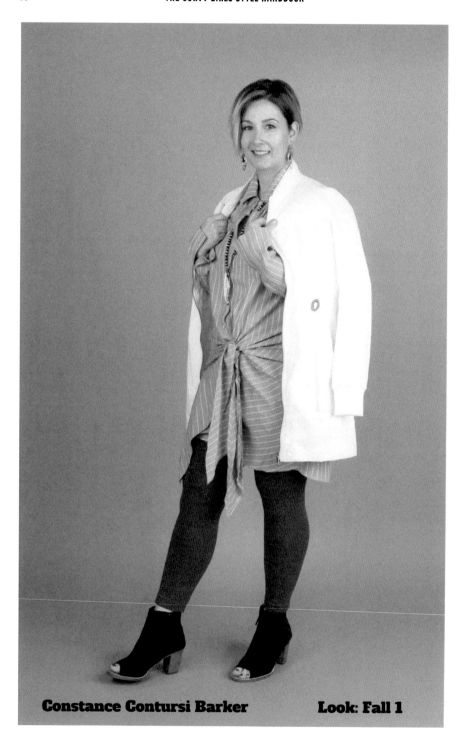

Constance Contursi Barker   **Look: Fall 1**

Outfit 1 Fall:

- Light blue stripe dress
- Grey leggings
- Quilted, white cargo jacket
- Black peep toe bootie
- Silver earrings, black and white beaded pendant necklace

Constance had not actually worn this adorable dress yet, and the jacket still had a price tag on it. She learned that by adding the layer of this cozy, white coat, could make for a fun fall ensemble. The quilted, canvas fabric and knit cuff suggest cooler months; forget about the old limiting saying that you can't wear white after Labor Day. That is just wrong. During the cold seasons, we switch out our light cotton, silks, and linens from spring and summer and reach for wools, furry and textured knits in the fall and winter. Constance could, for example, exchange the light leggings, for cropped, slim jeans in this outfit, and tall boots to transition it into winter.

The flattering bias cut of this dress, (where the fabric is cut on an angle) falls along the lines of her hips. In addition, a playful pleat opening and tie detail draw the eye into her body and highlights her waist. Remember the 'B', it is present here, and a naturally occurring 'V' is suggested by the button-down collar on the dress, and repeated by the black, white and silver, long pendant necklace.

Constance Contursi Barker   **Look: Winter**

Outfit 2 Winter:

- Khaki, embroidered tunic
- Magenta, faux motorcycle jacket
- Dark rinse, denim skinny jeans
- Tan, chunk heel mules
- Floral scarf
- Bold, gold earrings

Navigating the season change to winter is no problem when you are well stocked with the right pieces. The embroidery on this silky, khaki long top is so whimsical; I insisted we include it in our line-up. It instantly speaks volumes about Constance's chic – quirky style. The **'V for victory'** shape is achieved instantly with the button down and scarf accent.

Another closet basic, the motorcycle jacket is so fun in this bright magenta color, complementing the top. The shade of pink is repeated again in the scarf, creating cohesion. We found a long, woven, rope - belt with tassels and wrapped it twice to create a focal point at her waist, the **'B'**.

The lug sole on Constance's platform ankle boots give a masculine contrast to her feminine curves, and the tan suede plays nicely with the stitching in the top, belt and gold jewelry. In addition, she could layer a fur vest in tan tones, onto this look; for the warmth of course, but also for a nod to the bohemian look.

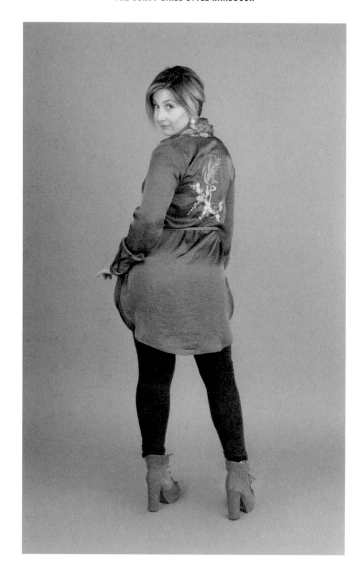

Constance Contursi Barker **Look: Spring**

<u>Outfit 3 Spring:</u>

- Floral sleeveless top
- Grey long cardigan
- Destroyed skinny jeans
- Light grey open toe bootie
- Bold silver earrings

A floral print does not technically have to be frilly flowers; it can be abstract or slightly graphic, like this top on Constance. The hues are made muted by the grey background, which help to ground it together with the long cardigan, also called a duster.

Now, the shape of the peplum top provides the perfect hourglass structure for Constance to highlight her small waist, **'B for Beltline'.** It is also extremely comfortable and easy to wear, as she doesn't have to worry about tucking anything into her playful, ripped, skinny jeans. Open-toe shoes have got be the best thing about spring, very liberating; show off that fresh, pretty pedicure!

Constance Contursi Barker **Look: Summer**

Outfit 4 Summer:

- Tan, white and black striped jumpsuit
- Black, faux leather moto jacket
- Blue suede, peep toe wedge - mules
- Bold, colorful J. Crew necklace

Constance is embracing her inner femme fatal with a wide leg pant, also called a palazzo pant, in this sporty and sexy jumpsuit. We emphasize an hourglass shape by using the **'Victory'** shape here on her neckline, and the **'B'**, self -belted waistline of the jumpsuit. It is further defined by the bomber jacket adding structure to her shoulders, and balanced by the wide width of the pant at the bottom. Bring a dash of 70's sophistication with this fun garment type; including the sharp, linear stripe print, it practically shouts confidence.

The bold royal blue, suede mules and bright necklace create a fun pop of color in an otherwise neutral outfit. Gold tones are the best choice in jewelry to compliment the warm tan and cream stripe fabric.

Lastly, a black leather or faux leather jacket – need I say more? Another must-have layering piece for your wardrobe, it really does go with anything.

Constance Contursi Barker   **Look: Fall 2**

Outfit 5 Fall again: (we couldn't stop ourselves)

- White print top
- Khaki green military jacket
- Black skinny pants
- Tan, chunk heel mules
- Chunky gold necklace

While a skinny pant can be a great wardrobe basic, they do require a balance of volume on the top, like a tunic style top, as we show on Constance. The classic Navajo pattern is revived in this slightly edgy print. It layers nicely under a classic military-inspired, lightweight jacket; also a wardrobe must-have, as it can be paired with so many things.

We created the '**Victory**' shape by opening the neck hole slightly and letting the ties fall down. She could do a half tuck of the top into her pants to give her more definition at her waist, creating the '**B for beltline**', or just leave it out, either way, she looks amazing!

The tan mules tie together the print in the top and the jewelry. I suggest finding at least two ways to tie a color scheme together. If you can incorporate three and four times to repeat colors, it just makes the outfit look more put together.

CHAPTER 4: A FEW WORDS ON ACCESSORIES

M ajor mood lifters, accessories can provide a little or a big refresh to your wardrobe, by creating 'new' looks from your clothing without having to overhaul your entire closet from season to season. Accessories are the magic addition to help complete an outfit and achieve the connecting visual needed via color, pattern, and texture.

I have a whole accessories section, called 'the top three' choices in the categories of shoes, handbags, and jewelry, in my first book: 'The T-Shirt & Jeans Handbook'. If you are unsure where to even begin with your accessory collection, and how to wear them, this is a good place to go.

I would like to offer a few tips here, however. Balance is a key component in how to wear accessories. One suggestion is to choose a focal point with your look and accessorize around it. When you are deciding which pieces to pair together, ie: earrings, necklace or both, take a look at the focal point of your outfit. Where is your eye drawn? If your eye is tracking to the top of the outfit, at the neckline, this is your focal point. In this scenario, you could balance a large necklace with a small earring, post or hoop, and vice-a-versa applies; a big earring with a smaller necklace, or no necklace at all.

Below is a list of what I like to call a hero piece; one item that can carry a whole outfit. It's vital to work with the wardrobe pieces you adore most and maximize each item to make fabulous outfits to wear on repeat.

Whether dressing for the work week or casual for the weekend, these items you can rely on for an elevated ensemble. As I always try to make clear, amazing personal style and cost of pieces are not mutually exclusive.

Mix your high and low, ie: your grandmother's pearls with something you bought from the Banana Republic, or your local boutique. Please, do not save the 'good stuff'!

Add one or more of these accessories for a quick wardrobe update.

Top 6 Accessories:

1. Belts:

Define your shape and add a finishing touch, with a thin, stylish belt, versatile neutrals are a must: brown, black and metallic. These trusty accessories complement jeans and trouser pants, while a fashion-forward option gives dresses and skirts a polished look. It's helpful to have a variety of thickness, lengths, and materials.

2. Block heal shoe, mule or ankle boot:

I gave up on stilettos decades ago. A square block shape heel is made for strutting, giving a little lift without the back and foot pain. Choose an open-toe version for spring and summer.

3. Silk scarf:

A large 36 inch square shape, or long rectangle (my favorite) scarves are highly useful all year around; silk fabrics never fail to look chic and luxurious.

If you're going the affordable route, a dark color pallet will ensure an opulent effect.

4. Basket-type handbag or clutch:

Woven straw, raffia or hemp, these timeless handbags are hard-working staples, especially for spring through fall. Trade in a metallic leather version for winter.

5. A chunky necklace, gold or silver:

One of these can literally be paired with anything from a fancy dress to a simple white T-shirt. Be careful with your choice, inexpensive metals can easily look ... inexpensive.

6. Metal tank watch:

Classic in every form, created in 1917 by Louis Cartier, this watch collection has become a legend and has inspired countless variations. I love wearing mine with everything from caftans to distressed jeans; it's a men's version, my husband gave me on our wedding day.

Tip: you cannot go wrong with the many different shades of silver, gold, copper and oxidized metallic leather accessories, and metal accents; for shoes, belts, and handbags, they are a refreshing change-up from black and brown.

Check out the fun line up of shoes from the photo shoot!

Two words on necklaces: color and texture.

CHAPTER 5: UNDERWEAR

O k, let's go there. Our wardrobe is incomplete without a trusted line up of undergarments and sleepwear. Beautiful lingerie can help us feel more sensual, sultry and sexy.

BRAS:

The wrong bra, however, or wrong size bra, can instantly destroy an otherwise awesome outfit; as well as potentially cause pain, back problems, and unnecessary suffering.

There are different naming conventions for a bra cup size larger than a D. Cup sizes larger than a D are called different letters by different brands (a DDD cup size in one brand can be called an E or F in other brands).

The best way to figure out the fit on any garment, especially under-garments, is by using a soft tape measure. Start with one of these, one of your best fitting bras, and a mirror.

Start by finding your band measurement, place the tape on the location around your rib cage, where your bra band rests. Then wrap the measuring tape around the circumference of the widest part of your beasts. If you have an odd number, round up. Subtract the band measurement from the bust measurement, and you have your cup size. Every number difference is one cup size, for example, a 40-inch band and a 49-inch bust would equal a 40H.

Check out this video for fitting instructions:

ME Majamas Bra Fit guide

TOP THREE BRA CHOICES:

1. T-Shirt Bra

The hardest working bra in your line-up, With a sleek, molded cup design, this bra is unobstructed by seams, or textures (like lace); a perfect complement to any garment, especially T-Shirts, or those with thin fabrics.

2. Sports Bra

I have heard of women who must wear two bras just to work out without bounce and pain. The best way to reduce rebound is to opt for an underwire design that completely encapsulates the breast tissue.

3. Sleep Bra

A busty Girl's best friend. A wireless style that provides support when sleeping or relaxing can be more comfortable than going bra free. It can also prevent sagging and chaffing.

A few more notes on the subject. You can go wireless, in the form of a bralette; traditionally a wire-free bra made from stretchy lace, with less support and structure. One with more support can be great base layer providing a peek of fabric in the cleavage area. Lastly, a sexy push-up bra is another ancillary choice to include in your bra wardrobe.

KNICKERS

Thongs, briefs, cheekies, or a waterfall edge (my favorite) - a cross between a bikini and a brief, with no elastic on the leg hole, and don't forget boyshorts; this subject is highly personal. I suggest you find a choice that is comfortable for you, as long as no panty lines are visible.

There are a handful of brands and retailers that cater specifically to curvy figures, offering pieces with adequate support and coverage, while still looking stylish.

RESOURCES:

ME Majamas, lingerie and athleisure

Peach, lingerie: (use this link below to buy, you get 10$ off first order, and I get a store credit)

Cosabella, lingerie

Yummie lingerie

CHAPTER 6: SIZING STANDARDS

Or the lack of

Have you ever found yourself standing in a fitting room on the verge of tears when something does not fit? Wondering why the same size in one brand is completely different from the size you might wear in a myriad of others? One of the reasons might be Vanity Sizing.

Vanity Sizing, or size inflation, is the phenomenon of ready-to-wear clothing of the same size becoming bigger in physical size over time. Vanity sizing tends to occur where clothing sizes are not standardized, such as in the U.S. market. Although clothing size standards exist, i.e., ASTM (1), most companies no longer use them.

Size inconsistency has existed since at least the 1940's. In a Sears catalog, of that time, a size 14 dress had a bust size of 32" (81 cm). In 1967, the same bust size was a size 8; in 2011, it was a size 0.

In 2003, a study that measured over 1,000 pairs of women's trousers found that pants from more expensive brands tended to be smaller than those from cheaper brands with a similar size.

In any event, it is important to know that American sizing, in particular, is completely arbitrary and unstandardized.

What makes these inconsistencies so insidious is that it becomes very difficult to pinpoint your actual size in any given garment, even within a particular manufacturer or brand, these numbers can vary.

My Solution: get a tape measure. Get to know which brands construction and size for each garment type fit your body, and try to buy from just those brands.

Size Chart: Wikipedia

Misses' sizes (ASTM D5585 11e1)[11] (2011)

5'5½" tall

Dimension/size	00	0	2	4	6	8	10	12	14	16	18	20
Bust	31⅛	31¾	33	34⅛	35¼	36¼	37¼	38¾	40⅜	42⅛	44	46
Waist (Straight)	25⅜	26⅛	26⅞	27⅝	28½	29½	30½	32¼	34	36	38¼	40½
Waist (Curvy)	23⅞	24⅝	25⅜	26⅛	27	28	29	30¾	32½	34½	36¾	39
Hip (Straight)	33¼	33⅞	35⅛	36⅜	37½	38½	39½	41	42½	44¼	46	48
Hip (Curvy)	34	34⅝	35⅞	37⅛	38¼	39¼	40¼	41¾	43¼	45	46¾	48¾

(1) ASTM International is an international standards organization that develops and publishes voluntary consensus technical standards for a wide range of materials, products, systems, and services.

Let us make a pact and remove the importance we put into the number on a tag. The value of our bodies and our very selves is not a concept be quantified by a number. Certainly not when the industry randomly changes the measuring stick to suit their needs.

We must reinforce the positive message about clothing, and that the fit and cut of our clothing are what to focus on; that a number on a tag holds no power over us. It is a challenge, but it is imperative that we put aside the material way of thinking. And move into the space held by our spirits, only you can decide how you want to think and feel about your body.

CHAPTER 7: RETAILERS, DESIGNERS AND THE FASHION INDUSTRY

According to many studies, the average size for women in the U.S. is a 16 and 67 percent are size 14 and higher, so this is the new normal.

Just knowing where the average is can help a lot of women understand that they are not alone.

I believe that the apparel industry is beginning to appreciate these numbers, the revenue associated, and the knowledge that these statistics, and the women, aren't going away.

Every one of us deserves to have clothing fit well, both in style and measurements, and be widely available in beautiful fabrics and empowering silhouettes.

As with most widespread change, leaders are needed to chart a new path. With the help of several celebrities and famous designers championing the way, the progress, albeit slow, is inspiring.

Body-positive celebrities like Melissa McCarthy have launched their own line of clothing in order to make fashion more fun and accessible for consumers who wear above a size 12. McCarthy's line, carries an impressive range of options, from size 4 to size 28.

Both Prabal Gurung and Michael Kors regularly feature plus-size models on their runways. The latter also launched a collaboration with Lane Bryant, offering pieces in sizes 10 - 28.

Honore, a new and dynamic Los Angeles-based e-commerce site specializes in designer clothing for sizes 10 through 20.

Nicolette Mason and Gabi Gregg are two of the most successful personal style Editors and Bloggers, who as plus-size women, faced a common challenge of finding the kind of trend-forward clothes they wanted to wear and write about. The duo recently debuted their collection for their online platform called Premme, in an effort to share the same passion to create those kinds of clothes and looks for their audience.

The creators of Premme believe that clothing should be about expressing your personality, having fun, and not feeling limited by our culture and society's fashion rules. Their lines bring a whole new point of view to the market with attention worthy and affordable pieces available in a range of sizes from 12 to 30.

Project Runway alumni, Christian Siriano has also been especially proactive about bringing needed change to the industry. He has held body positive runway shows and spoken out about his decision to dress plus-size celebrities for the red carpet.

Below is a list of Designers and Retailers who are producing super chic garments for our curvy - body sisters:

SHOPPING RESOURCES:

Honoré, e-commerce site, specializes in designer clothing (size 10 – 20)

Preme, e-commerce site

ME Majamas, lingerie and athleisure

Dia & CO. – monthly clothing subscription box size (14 – 32)

Melissa McCarthy for Nordstrom & Macy's, Amazon & ShopStyle

Prabal Gurung for Lane Bryant (size 10 – 28)

Haute & Co., Chicago Bridal Salon (size 14 – 28)

ASOS Curve & Plus Size

Beyond by Ashley Graham, for Dress Barn

Torrid, size 10-30 online and in-store, Women's Jeans, Spring & Summer Dresses, Activewear, Workwear

Peggy Goodman Collections, jewelry in this book. Use the code curvygirl20 to get 20% off

Instagram:

@Shop.kahaari

@Shopreadytostare Body Positive Accessories + Apparel by fashion Blogger, Alysse Dalessandro

CHAPTER 8: BODY IMAGE AND SELF ESTEEM

It's deeper than the clothes

Which leads me to my next chapter. Body image is an intellectual or idealized image of what one's body is or should look like. It can be misconceived and influenced by the comments and reactions we received from family and friends, our culture and society, as well as the fashion industry and the media. Body image has a deep and lasting impact on our physical, mental, and emotional well-being. Think about that Crossfitter, who in the same day can experience the joy of a new personal record in a back squat, powered by her powerful quads; to hating her thighs because she can't find a pair of slacks that are proportioned for her.

Negative body image can lead to low self- esteem, depression, illness and life-threatening disorders. Ninety percent of women and young girls say they do not feel represented in the fashion industry or in media, and that the imagery they absorb on a daily basis makes them feel 'less than' or 'disgusting'.

The documentary Straight/Curve examines the various industries and obstacles responsible for this body image crisis and showcases the dynamic leaders fighting for more diversity of size, age, and race.

Our brain processes images 60,000 times faster than words, Straight/Curve sets out to change the mental images we are seeing and to bolster a movement that is redefining society's unrealistic and dangerous standards of beauty to impact our society at large.

Aesthetic comes in all sorts of shapes, colors, and sizes; spiritually, mentally, emotionally, as well as physically. We humans have a deep desire for a beautiful aesthetic in all things. We seek it out instinctually, finding it in nature, a work of art, a wonderful meal, or a piece of music. This concept of beauty also transcends the physical: acts of kindness, the gratitude of a loved one, a display of courage, the list is endless.

The famous last lines of the poem, Ode on a Grecian Urn, by John Keats states: 'Beauty is truth, truth is beauty'. I like this, but what does it mean? It has been interpreted many ways; perhaps beauty is an order, a relation of parts that form a whole greater than the sum of its parts. Truth speaks to the intellect, beauty to the emotions. But they are the same, in that they are both revelations of an existence which is larger than ourselves.

Believe and know that you are beautiful and of value, exactly as you are; I believe in you.

I have worked diligently to understand and appreciate myself, my gifts and my value. I would like to suggest a few ways to shift, and align with a higher vibrational self-esteem related to a poor body image and learn to love your body.

Tune into your thoughts and actions. A non-material, or no-ego method to consider: the body is a container for your soul, here on this planet to accomplish the spiritual goal of fulfilling your purpose. A healthy and strong body can accomplish these goals, so feed it the kinds of rich, nourishing foods it needs to do so, treat it with the love and respect it deserves.

Everything changes once we understand that we are not just physical beings in a physical body, that we are energetic beings in an energetic body; one of our challenges is learning to transmit vibrations to radiate and attract naturally what we want.

Vibrational self and thoughts attract compatible patterns. Identify and produce a higher vibration of signals, such as happiness, joy, positive loving relationships, financial abundance, and a healthy, strong body. Embody these feelings and you will attract more of it to you. This will help you to fall in love with who you really are on the inside and will traction toward the outside.

Go for a run, sing your favorite song, meditate, take an epsom salt bath - to get out of old patterns of negative or low vibrational signals. The goal is to move toward the feelings states you want to create, the new patterns of thinking you wish, that are compatible with your desires.

It can be difficult sometimes to see yourself with kind eyes, especially if you've ever tried to lose weight before and failed. But when you can learn how to see yourself in a different light and change your self-image, this will contribute to living a healthy, happy and extraordinary life.

For over a millennium, ancient philosophers have taught us that each person is born with a unique gift, one that can help or serve others. Once you free yourself from any kind of blockage, for example, body blocks, money or relationship ones, you can be fully present to your purpose on the planet.

Check out my most referred APPs and programs for finding aware-ness, balance, empathy, and expansion:

1. The Change Militia: a self - guided system, with weekly zoom 'live' calls, to stop overwhelm and feelings of being stagnant. Join a group of strong, curious, and passionate people, practicing movements and concepts, to help you get unstuck, feel happy, content, fulfilled, play-ful, powerful and focus on being increasingly kind.

2. Insight Timer: meditation app, with access to 10,000 different guided meditations, music, teachings and talks.

CHAPTER 9: AFFIRMATIONS OF SELF

Love and empowerment

Affirmations are short, but powerful, confirming statements which describe a goal, or desire in a completed state. The more you can feel for these desired outcomes, the higher probability you will achieve them. An affirmation is powerful because it has the ability to program your mind and body into believing and applying the stated concept.

Our internal dialogue, self- talk if you will, is a steady stream of affirmations. We are in fact, using affirmations every moment whether aware of it know it or not. We're affirming and creating our life experiences with every word and thought.

Beliefs are merely habitual thinking patterns that have been learned as a child.

Awareness is the key here, start listening to the language you use to talk about yourself and others and remove the thoughts and words that do not serve your goals. It's all about knowing you are whole, complete, beautiful; tuning into and feeling the emotions you want right now in the present moment. This includes the awareness that whatever you want to manifest is because you believe you will feel better when you have it.

Why am I talking about this, in a book about style? Well, I believe that how we feel about ourselves is the key to confidence and rocking an amazing outfit is the method I use, and teach my clients to use, to achieve this outcome.

I have discovered the power of affirmations and use them every day as a part of my morning routine. They change periodically; I write them down on note cards and tape the cards to my bathroom mirror, so I can read them in the morning. It's something that has helped me overcome pesky habits and negative thoughts that don't serve me, like self-doubt, fear, and demand. These love notes, as I sometimes call them, can play a huge role in your journey to love and acceptance of yourself inside and out.

Once I changed my mindset, with the help of these little phrases, the world around me changed. I learned to recognize that I am already whole and complete, that I was born that way – full of value and potential. I learned to love my body and myself fully, even my stretch marks, cellulite, and now, my wrinkles.

Some of the most powerful affirmations follow these two words: I am. To make this work, you must truly feel in your body, mind, and spirit that which you wish to make happen, and the manifestation will happen. It's a scientific law of quantum physics: state your desire, believe and feel for that vibration and take action.

Here are mine; I speak them while looking at myself in the mirror:

I am enough

I am fearless

I am kind to myself

I am loved

I am already whole and complete

I am ecstatic

I am successful

I am financially stable

I have no demands

I am cosmically charged

I am fabulous

I am enough (this one bears repeating, it is so important)

You can start to harness the power of affirmations by using this exercise and writing about the things you value, like your family or your career, or even a sunny and warm, spring day in Chicago

CHAPTER 10: LOVE YOUR CLOSET CHECK LIST

Creating and maintaining an oasis for getting dressed every day will not only bring you joy and happiness, it will help you be more creative with your things and save you precious time and energy.

At the beginning of each new season, especially spring and fall, you can find a myriad of blogs, off and online magazine articles on cleaning out your closet. There are books, some even household names, encouraging us to purge and live more simply with less stuff.

Overwhelm can squash all good intentions of a closet clean up; what I suggest you do is start with three easy steps to help you update your wardrobe for any changing season. If you are a 'get things done – proactive' personality, by all means, choose a weekend and have at it. If not, take one task and let yourself complete it slowly over one or two weeks, there is no need to kill yourself.

1. Reign in excess. This is not always easily done on your own, however imperative for maintaining order and sanity:

- Remove items that are wrong sized, do not fit, unclean and in disrepair.
- Organize by color, then category; this makes outfit building easier, as you can then find everything and be more daring in making new combinations.

2. Update your space:

- A fresh coat of paint in a vivid hue, like royal blue (what I chose for my closet), a cozy area rug and full - length mirror are simple touches creating a personal space inspiring you to dress and feel fabulous for every occasion. If you have the square footage include seating, my small round ottoman from HomeGoods is also used for reaching handbags on the high shelves.

3. Invest in organizing tools:

- Buy a valet hook. Hang one of these on the back of a closet or bathroom door, or nail it on the wall. This invaluable device will save you time by providing a place and encouraging a process for staging outfits.
- A wall hanging or counter sitting, jewelry rack is a must have to ensure your lovely pieces stay untangled and openly viewable, so you can wear them more often, mixing fine jewelry with your fashion jewelry collection.
- Shelving or a rack for shoes is imperative to treating your shoes beautifully and being able to see everything you have. I had an oddly shaped closet from an addition we put in our house, so I hired a contractor to install shoe shelves. They work perfect for me, as they are very deep, allowing me to move the current season forward and the offseason shoes to the back.

- Check out The Bangle Stacker. Use code Curvy and get 20% off your purchase!

THE TEAM

A heartfelt thanks to:

THE PHOTOGRAPHER

Meka Hemmons, super pro photographer, owner of Spider Meka Photography.

It was truly an insightful, soulful experience to work with Meka. Her immeasurable talent and vision have created the most beautiful images, I could not have imagined. Read her thoughts below on why she is doing what she does. Her philosophy is in complete alignment with this project and explains exactly why I wanted to work with Meka.

Meka's mission:

My heart breaks when I hear women speak negatively about their natural features, or complain about those "extra" pounds. Women are the nurturers in the community – we do so much for others that we forget to take care of ourselves, and when we do think of ourselves, we say too many things about how we're not good enough, not fortunate enough, or not pretty enough.

I spent 20 years making celebrities flawless for magazine spreads, regularly asked to de-humanize proportions and textures. Natural beauty is far more interesting and appealing than some of the images I was asked to produce. I've embraced the study of lighting, posing, and styling to now share the truth of how a combination of these three simple things is all that's needed to bring out how uniquely breathtaking you are.

Why NOT now? Our culture has been brainwashed long enough with beauty being some supernatural quality. Working with one of the most influential persons on the planet definitely gave me the right perspective to not fear moving forward when your heart is in the right place and you have the opportunity to do what you love. All of life's experiences culminate to this very moment. Let the past propel you onward to greater things.

THE MODELS

I would like to share a little more information on my super models.

DENISE WALSH

Denise is an Entrepreneur and expert in sales/merchandising and strategic/management for retailers. Her passion is helping women feel their best with confidence by providing long lasting, anti -aging skin care and cosmetics products by Senegence. Visit her site: www.senegence.com/dazzlinglipsbydenise

STACY SAUNDERS

Stacey is owner of <u>Saunders Consulting</u>, a productivity firm for small business owners in Chicago.

CONSTANCE COURSI BARKER

About Constance's business:

Hit It!® Fitness offers effective and innovative group exercise classes

which are programmed according to each individual's needs, preferences and fitness level. Her team offers private personal training, clean eating "real-food" nutrition coaching and have a line of workout DVDs. She is a national master trainer and continuing education provider for fitness pros all around the country.

Many thanks to Kyle Hanson for the cover art.

A special thanks to Joe Solari:

The ungodly, endless hours, and early - rising days this man spent to get his own work competed as well as research and support my projects. It's hard to put into words how much respect, love an appreciation I have for Joe. Smart, funny and devoted, I could not ask for a more amazing partner in business and in life.

Lucky me. But then, I manifested him, did I not?

Joe is a traditional Business Consultant, and author of The Business Owner's Compendium, with a focus on small and medium size companies - operations, digital marketing and self publishing.

ABOUT THE AUTHOR

Suze Solari is a Personal Style Consultant, a fashion contributor for a Chicago newspaper, and author of the Stylish Upgrades books series: The T- Shirt & Jeans Handbook and The Blouse & Skirt Handbook, on iBooks, Kobo & Amazon. She works with clients nationwide, and is known for helping them maximize their wardrobe investment and learn to wear the right pieces to achieve their goals and be the best version of themselves.

Sign up to receive the newsletter and get a free PDF copy of my first book.

 twitter.com/suzstyl

 instagram.com/suzstyl

ALSO BY SUZE SOLARI

The T-Shirt & Jeans Handbook

The Blouse & Skirt Handbook

Affiliate Link Notice:

Included in the book are a few links where I am paid a fee or receive store credit if you become a customer. This comes out of the sellers profit and in some cases you receive a discount or special deal.

These are ones that I have used in the past and endorse:

ME Majamas

The Change Militia

Peach Lingerie

Bangle Stacker

I spend a lot of time hunting down items for clients who have a difficult time finding clothing that works for them. I want you to have the benefit of this research and to send business to some of the smaller brands who are trying to do right by you and the environment.

Made in the USA
Middletown, DE
20 November 2019